American Symbols

The American Flag

By Lloyd G. Douglas

SCHOLASTIC INC.

New York Toronto London Auckland Sydney
Mexico City New Delhi Hong Kong Buenos Aires

ISBN 0-516-24484-1

12 11 10 9 8 7 6 5 4 3 2 1   3 4 5 6 7 8/0

Printed in the U.S.A.   61

First Scholastic paperback printing, September 2003

Contents

The American **flag** is a **symbol** of the United States.

It was chosen on June 14, 1777.

5

There were thirteen red and white **stripes** on the first American flag.

The stripes stood for the thirteen states that made up the country.

7

There were thirteen stars on the first American flag, too.

Each star also stood for a state.

9

The American flag has been **changed** many times.

More stars were added to the flag when more states were added to the country.

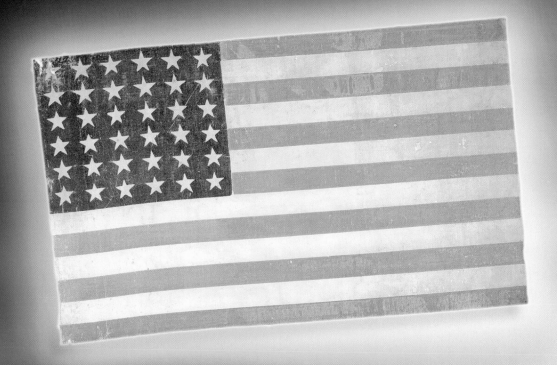

Today, there are fifty stars on the American flag.

The fifty stars stand for the fifty states in the United States of America.

13

There are still thirteen stripes on the American flag.

The stripes now stand for the first thirteen **colonies** in America.

June 14 is Flag Day.

People have **parades** to **celebrate** the American flag.

Many people put the American flag on their houses.

The flag shows that they **support** America.

People have put the American flag in many places.

It is even on the moon!

The American flag is an important symbol of America.

21

New Words

celebrate (**sel**-uh-brate) to do something enjoyable on a special occasion

changed (**chaynjd**) having made something different from the way it was before

colonies (**kol**-uh-neez) lands that have been settled by people from another country

flag (**flag**) a piece of cloth that has different shapes and colors on it

parades (puh-**raydz**) groups of people walking down streets

stripes (**stripes**) lines of color that are next to different colors

support (suh-**port**) to believe in or favor something

symbol (**sim**-buhl) an object that represents something else

To Find Out More

Web Site
Kid's Domain: Flag Day
http://www.kidsdomain.com/holiday/flagday
Learn about Flag Day and find fun activities to do on this Web site.

Index

About the Author
Lloyd G. Douglas is an editor and writer of children's books.

Reading Consultants
Kris Flynn, Coordinator, Small School District Literacy, The San Diego County Office of Education

Shelly Forys, Certified Reading Recovery Specialist, W.J. Zahnow Elementary School, Waterloo, IL

Sue McAdams, Former President of the North Texas Reading Council of the IRA, and Early Literacy Consultant, Dallas, TX